The TITHE
A test in trust

by Larry Kreider

House to House Publications
Ephrata, Pennsylvania USA

The Tithe: A Test In Trust
Larry Kreider

Copyright © 1996
Updated Edition 2003
House To House Publications
1924 West Main Street, Ephrata, PA 17522 USA
Telephone: (717) 738-3751
Fax: (717) 738-0656
Web site: www.dcfi.org

ISBN 1-886973-17-2

Unless otherwise noted, all scripture quotations in this publication are taken from the *Holy Bible, New International Version* (NIV).
© 1973, 1978, 1984 by International Bible Society. Used by permission of Zondervan Publishing House. All rights reserved.

All rights reserved. No portion of this book may be reproduced without the permission of the publisher.

The Tithe
A test in trust

A Christian friend of mine visited a non-believing friend one weekend and asked his friend to attend church with him. My friend recalls how embarrassed he was when he realized the purpose of the service that Sunday morning was to collect money to purchase a new organ. They began to ask for pledges—thousand dollar pledges, five-hundred dollar pledges, and one-hundred dollar pledges. In fact, it took the entire meeting to prod and beg the people to make pledges. The non-Christian friend was so disillusioned by what he experienced that he never wanted to return to church!

Many Christians have an unhealthy understanding of finances. They have been conditioned to give out of a sense of duty or obligation. That is not what giving and tithing to the Lord is about! Giving should come out of a sense of faith in God's grace (2 Corinthians 8:1-4); it should never be done grudgingly or out of a sense of compulsion. *Each man should give what he has de-*

cided in his heart to give, not reluctantly or under compulsion, for God loves a cheerful giver (2 Corinthians 9:7).

Scripture has a tremendous amount to say about money or material possessions. Sixteen of the thirty-eight parables of Jesus deal with money. One out of every ten verses in the New Testament addresses this subject. Scripture has 500 verses on prayer, and less than 500 verses on faith; but there's over 2,000 verses on the subject of money and material possessions. Money is such an important issue because a person's attitude toward it often reveals his relationship with God.

God wants to restore a healthy, godly understanding of finances in the body of Christ today. Let's be open to what God's Word says about finances.

Recognize God's Ownership In Everything

First and foremost, we must realize that everything we have belongs to God. We are merely stewards (managers) of any material goods we possess. God owns everything we have, but He makes us managers of it. *Let a man so consider us, as servants of Christ and stewards of the mysteries of God. Moreover it is required in stewards that one be found faithful. And what do you have that you did not receive...? (1 Corinthians 4:1-2,7b NKJ).*

When my wife, LaVerne, and I served as missionaries, we had the job of buying the food and supplies for the other missionaries at our base each week. The money we were using was not our own; we were simply managing it. It belonged to the mission board.

I shared this principle of being a manager of God's money in Nairobi, Kenya, one time, and it made complete sense to one of the ladies in the audience. She told me that, as a bank teller, she understood that even though she handles massive amounts of money daily, the money is not hers. It belongs to the bank. She is simply a manager.

I am a manager of the Lord's money. In reality, the money in my wallet is not mine; it is God's. Some Christians believe that ten percent of the money they receive is God's and the other ninety percent belongs exclusively to them. They are mistaken. It *all* belongs to God. We need to recognize His ownership in everything we have:

...for everything in heaven and earth is yours...wealth and honor come from you...(1 Chronicles 29:11b,12a).

"The silver is mine and the gold is mine," declares the Lord Almighty (Haggai 2:8).

For every animal of the forest is mine, and the cattle on a thousand hills (Psalms 50:10).

While LaVerne and I served as missionaries, I drove a van owned by the mission, and although I sensed responsibility for the van, I realized that it did not belong to me. Ultimately, it belonged to God. It was a good lesson in managing someone else's property that is similar to the responsibility God has given us to manage the wealth He has given us. God has given us a responsibility as managers of His wealth. It all belongs to Him. We have to stop thinking like owners, and start thinking like managers.

God Associates Our Ability to Handle Money With Our Ability to Handle Spiritual Things

Did you know God associates our ability to handle money with our ability to handle spiritual matters? One day Jesus made some amazing statements regarding this principle. *Whoever can be trusted with very little can also be trusted with much, and whoever is dishonest with very little will also be dishonest with much. So if you have not been trustworthy in handling worldly wealth, who will trust you with true riches? And if you have not been trustworthy with someone else's property, who will give you property of your own? No servant can serve two masters. Either he will hate the one and love the other, or he will be devoted to the one and despise the other. You cannot serve both God and Money (Luke 16:10-13).*

Money, in terms of true value, is a "little" thing. However, faithfulness in little things (money) indicates our faithfulness in big things (spiritual values). Jesus said that those who are not trustworthy in the use of their worldly wealth will be the same with spiritual things. Jesus said that we cannot serve two masters—God and materialism. It is impossible to hold allegiance to two masters at the same time.

Being surrounded with the world's riches may give us a false sense of security. Christians must not hold on too tightly to possessions because they have a way of deceiving us and demanding our hearts' loyalty. How we handle finances often is a reflection or indicator of our hearts. The Lord is very concerned with our use of finances because He knows that if He can trust us with finances, He can trust us with spiritual things.

When God Blesses Us Financially, He is Taking A Risk

It amazes me to see how God constantly takes risks on His creation. When God created the angels, He took a risk. The archangel, Lucifer (Satan), tried to exalt himself above the Lord, so God had to throw him out of heaven (Isaiah 14:12-17). When God created mankind, giving us free wills, He took a risk.

Did you know that every time God blesses us financially, He is taking a risk? He takes a risk with you and me when He asks us to be stewards (managers) of His finances and material possessions, because we may begin to serve money instead of serving the true God. God, at times, blessed Israel with wealth as a sign that He was fulfilling His covenant. *But remember the Lord your God, for it is he who gives you the ability to produce wealth...(Deuteronomy 8:18).* We should expect financial blessings from the Lord. God wants us to be fruitful.

However, with the blessing of wealth, the Lord instructed His people to be careful so that they did not forget the Lord their God. God knows that our tendency is to allow money to be our God. We must remember that our lives do not consist in the abundance of the things that we possess...*Watch out! Be on your guard against all kinds of greed; a man's life does not consist in the abundance of his possessions (Luke 12:15).*

In the first of the Ten Commandments, the Lord commands us to "have no other gods before Him." The last commandment says we should not "covet what belongs to our neighbors." To *covet* means *to desire enviously that which belongs to another.* If we covet others' financial blessings, we are putting money ahead of God. Material possessions do not give life to us. Only a relationship with Jesus produces life! We must not allow material wealth to distract us from our heavenly calling.

Giving Keeps us From Materialism and Helps Expand God's Kingdom

Although God wants to bless us materially, it should not be our focus. *People who want to get rich fall into temptation and a trap and into many foolish and harmful desires that plunge men into ruin and destruction (1 Timothy 6:9).*

The Lord does not want us to have money on our minds all the time. Materialism is a preoccupation with material rather than spiritual things. Our primary focus should be on the kingdom of God, not on money. However, it does take money to expand the kingdom of God. We should not be a slave to money because God's purpose for money is for it to be a servant to us. Money is for purchasing the necessities of life and giving to those in need and to finance the spread of the kingdom of God. This bears repeating: The real purpose for receiving God's prosperity is to expand the kingdom of God.

Giving keeps us from materialism. Giving breaks the power of money to become an idol in our lives. God wants to bless us so we can sow into His kingdom and help the poor.

To be blessed financially simply means we have all that we need to meet the needs in our lives, and an abundance left over to give to others. The purpose for having a job and working should be for...*doing something useful with [our] his own hands, that [we] he may have something to share with those in need (Ephesians 4:28b).*

When we diligently work and faithfully give of our finances, the Bible teaches that God "will meet all our needs according to His glorious riches" (Philippians 4:19). He wants to meet our needs and enable us to meet the needs of others. God promises to take care of us. He wants to bless and prosper us! If you are a businessman, an employee, a student or a housewife, the Lord desires to prosper you. Remember, God revealed Himself to Abraham as *El Shaddai*...the *God of more than enough*. He promised to bless Abraham abundantly, just as He desires to meet our needs and abundantly bless us in every way today. Giving really does keep us from getting materialistic.

Misconceptions

Christians may fall into one of two camps when it comes to what they believe is God's perspective regarding a Christian's financial life-style—some may take the viewpoint that all Christians should be poor and others may take the viewpoint that all Christians should be rich.

Those who believe all Christians should be rich often believe financial wealth is a clear sign of God's blessing. However, God's "blessing" cannot *always* be equated with personal material gain. It involves so much more! God certainly wants to bless us financially. He wants to bless us in every way. *Dear friend, I pray that you may enjoy good health and that all may go well with you, even as your soul is getting along well (3 John 1:2).*

However, if we believe, like the Pharisees did, that great wealth is a *sign* of God's favor, we will look down on people who are poor. The Pharisees looked down on Jesus for being financially poor (Luke 16:14). But Jesus did not do the same. In fact, we see that the people of the church at Smyrna were destitute, yet Jesus said they were spiritually rich (Revelation 2:8-10). Although God wants to prosper us in every way, including financially, financial wealth does not necessarily mean we are blessed by God. The Laodicean Christians were a case in point. Scripture tells us they were wealthy, yet they were considered spiritually "wretched" (Revelation 3:17).

On the other hand, many wealthy people *are* blessed by God because they use their finances unselfishly. Job was a rich and godly man who did not allow his money to become his god (Genesis 13:2). Abraham also had great wealth and was very godly (Job 1). Before he had an encounter with Jesus, Zacchaeus, a wealthy tax collector, trusted his riches instead of trusting in the living God. But after he met Jesus, he gave back four times what he had taken from others (Luke 19:8).

In the other camp, and often in reaction to the very seductive power of money in our lives, some believers take the viewpoint that all Christians should be poor. They often have a fear of what money can do to them. They fear its corrupting influence and believe money will cause them to backslide. Some may have been wounded by financial scandals in the church and now reject any kind of wealth as having an evil influence.

Cutting through the smoke of the two opposing viewpoints, the truth remains. The Lord is not for or against money; it has no morality to Him. Money is amoral in and of itself. It is *what we do with it* and *our attitude toward it* that makes it moral or immoral.

Money is not the root of evil like some people like to misquote in 1 Timothy 6:10. In this scripture, the Lord warns us to beware of the pitfall of *loving* money. It is the *love* of money that is a root of all kinds of evil. *For the love of money is a root of all kinds of evil. Some people, eager for money, have wandered from the faith and pierced themselves with many griefs (1 Timothy 6:10).*

We can be lovers of money, whether we have little or much. It depends on what we are placing our affections in. Rich or poor, if we begin to love money, it will lead us down the path of greed and cause much pain in our lives and in the lives of those around us.

A Bill to God: Giving a Portion of Our Income

The Lord gives us the responsibility to manage the resources He gives to us. He has set up a system to constantly remind us of His ownership in everything. This systematic way to give is a first step to allowing our resources to be used for God's kingdom.

In the Old Testament, the Israelites were required to give one-tenth of all their income to the Lord. The Hebrew word for *tithe* means *a tenth part*. At the very heart of tithing is the idea that God owns everything. God was simply asking the Israelites to return what He first gave them. *Honor the Lord with your wealth, with the firstfruits of all your crops; then your barns will be filled to overflowing, and your vats will brim over with new wine (Proverbs 3:9-10).*

We honor God by giving Him the "firstfruits" or a portion of our income. It shows that we honor Him as the Lord of all our possessions. This tithe (10%) opens up a way for God to pour out His blessings on us. Every time we give our tithes, we are reminded that all of our money and earthly possessions belong to God. We are simply stewards responsible for what the Lord has given us.

The word *tithe* is first mentioned in Genesis 14:18-20. *Then Melchizedek king of Salem brought out bread and wine. He was priest of God Most High, and he blessed Abram, saying, "Blessed be Abram by God Most High, Creator of heaven and earth. And blessed be God Most High, who delivered your enemies into your hand." Then Abram gave him a tenth of everything.*

Abraham gave Melchizedek a tithe before the Old Testament law had ever been written. Abraham was honoring the Lord and Melchizedek as the priest of the Most High God with ten percent of that which the Lord had given to him. He may have learned this principle from Abel who brought the firstborn of his flock to the Lord.

At the end of every month I face a stack of bills that I need to pay. One of these bills is my bill to God. It is called a *tithe*, my "firstfruit." This tithe reminds me that everything I have belongs to Him. I have learned to enjoy returning this 10% to the Lord. After all, Jesus has given to me 100% of Himself through His death on the cross. I am eternally grateful!

Robbing God

In the 1992 riots in Los Angeles, California, looting took place in many stores and businesses. A young man was asked by a reporter what he had stolen. He said, "I stole Christian tapes because I am a Christian." You might think that sounds ridiculous. Yet, in a similar way, there are many Christians who are stealing from God by keeping for themselves that which really belongs to the Lord—the tithe.

In Old Testament history, some of the Israelites were robbing God by selfishly holding onto money that belonged to God. They were required to give at least one-tenth of the livestock, the land's produce and their income to the Lord. In addition they were required to bring other offerings in the form of sacrifices or free-will offerings. But God says they were holding back. *"Will a man rob God? Yet you have robbed Me! But you say, 'In what way have we robbed You?' In tithes and offerings. You are cursed with a curse, for you have robbed Me, even this whole nation. Bring all the tithes into the storehouse, that there may be food in My house, and try Me now in this," says the Lord of hosts, "If I will not open for you the windows of heaven and pour out for you such blessing that there will not be room enough to receive it. And I will rebuke the devourer for your sakes, so that he will not destroy the fruit of your ground, nor shall the vine fail to bear fruit for you in the field," says the Lord of hosts (Malachi 3:8-11 NKJ).*

When the people asked God how they were robbing Him, He responded clearly, "In tithes and offerings." Notice, He not only tells us to bring "tithes," but also "offerings."

Many of God's people today are robbing God in this same way. The Lord has promised us that if we obey Him and bring all of our tithes into the storehouse, He will open the windows of heaven, pour out a blessing on us, and "rebuke the devourer." Many people are struggling financially because the devil has been robbing and devouring them. The enemy has not been rebuked by the Lord, because they are not paying tithes into the storehouse.

We are blessed as God rebukes the devourer when we tithe. However, our primary motivation for tithing should not be to get something back from God. Our primary motivation for tithing is obedience—to God and His Word.

I've known some people who have said that when they initially began to tithe, the enemy attacked them, and they found themselves worse off financially than ever before. The enemy may test us when we obey the Word of God. When Jesus was baptized, the heavens opened, and the Lord said, "This is my beloved Son in whom I am well pleased." During the next forty days of His life, Jesus was tested by the enemy. Tests will always come; however, if we hold on, we will receive the blessing that comes from obedience. God's promises always prove to be true!

When I was a missionary, the enemy tested me in the area of tithing. "You gave your entire life to God," he told me, "how could the Lord expect you to give back a tithe from the small amount of money you are receiving?" By the grace of God, I refused the enemy's lies and began to tithe even the small amount the Lord had provided for us. The Lord blessed us over and over again in a supernatural way as we served in the mission field. God is faithful. He honors His Word.

The Tithe Is A Numerical Expression That All I Have Belongs To God

The tithe is a numerical expression reminding us that all we have belongs to God. Some years ago, I was reading the book of

Malachi and was convicted by the Lord in the area of tithing. I checked my bank ledger. I had a whole list of bills. In fact, one of the bills I was delinquent in paying was my bill to God. Every month, my bill to God grew. I was not paying my tithe because I thought I did not have enough money to pay it.

One day, I made a decision to obey God. When I received my next paycheck, I paid all of my tithes to God. Some time later, I realized something supernatural had happened after I had taken this step of obedience. Our money seemed to last longer! The Lord began to provide for us financially, often in supernatural ways. It didn't happen overnight, but God began to bless us in a new way, and the devourer was rebuked.

Some people say, "I can't afford to tithe." The truth is—they cannot afford to withhold the tithe. A tithe is money set apart for God. If we don't give it to God, the devourer will consume it. Let's read again what God says in His Word about rebuking the devourer when we give tithes and offerings into His storehouse. *And I will rebuke the devourer for your sakes, so that he will not destroy the fruit of your ground, nor shall the vine fail to bear fruit for you in the field...(Malachi 3:11 NKJ).*

The word *devour* in the original Hebrew text means *to eat, burn up or consume.* During the days of Malachi, God's people were experiencing famine, scarcity, unseasonable weather, and insects that ate up the fruits of the earth. According to the above scripture, the enemy will devour our blessings when we choose to not obey God's principles. When we walk out from under the umbrella of protection of obedience to the Word of God concerning tithing, it gives the enemy a legal right to devour our blessings.

According to Webster's dictionary, *a tithe is 10% of one's income paid as a tax to the church.* When you pay your taxes to the government, do you *feel* like paying it? Do we have to *feel* like paying our tithe back to God? Of course not. Whether or not we *feel* like tithing is not the issue. We need to tithe in *obedience* to Him.

Imagine going to the bank and paying off a loan or a mortgage. How does the bank teller respond when we pay? Does she pat us on the back and tell us how much she appreciates it that we came to pay our bill? No, and neither should we expect God to pat us on the back when we tithe. We are not doing God any great favor when we tithe. It belongs to Him anyway. It is our responsibility to tithe, and we do it out of obedience.

Giving Systematically

The Lord wants us to learn to give systematically just like the believers were encouraged to do in 1 Corinthians 16:2. *On the first day of every week, each one of you should set aside a sum of money in keeping with his income, saving it up, so that when I come no collections will have to be made.*

Some believers claim to "follow the Spirit" as to when they will tithe. That's like calling your electric company and saying, "I'm not sure if I will pay my bill this month. Maybe I'll pay it next month. I'm just going to follow the Spirit." If you did not pay, you would get your electric service disconnected. We should always follow the Holy Spirit within the framework of the Word of God. The Word of God teaches us to tithe systematically as an act of obedience, not just when we feel like it.

Imagine giving your employer a phone call and telling him, "I will come to work when I think the Spirit is prompting me to come." Can you guess what would happen? You would probably lose your job! The same principle applies to giving to the Lord in a systematic way. Yes, we should follow the Spirit in our giving that is over and above our regular tithes. However, our God is a God of order and discipline. He instructs us to give tithes systematically so we do not have to "catch up on our giving" because we didn't give on a consistent basis.

Some believers say, "I think I'll pray about tithing." That's a bit like praying about whether or not we should read the Bible regularly or whether or not we should be part of a local church. These principles are clear in the Word of God, just like tithing.

I have been asked, "Should we tithe on the net (wages I receive after my taxes are paid) or the gross (wages I receive before the taxes are paid)?" When we pay your taxes to the government, do we pay taxes on the net or on the gross? We pay on whatever we have received (the gross amount). As Christians, we should desire to give everything we possibly can back to God because of what Jesus Christ has done for us. Remember, tithing is not an option. It is an act of obedience to God. It is a privilege to return to God what is already His.

Attitudes Toward Tithing

Sometimes Christians believe that tithing is simply an Old Testament doctrine. Dr. Bill Hamon says, "One divine principle in biblical interpretation is that whatever was established in the Old Testament remains proper as a principle or practice unless the New Testament does away with it. For instance, tithing was established in the Old Testament, but since nothing is stated in the New Testament that abolishes it, then it is still a proper practice for Christians."[1]

Jesus confirms the Old Testament principle of tithing in the New Testament. However, He does not want us to tithe with the attitude of the scribes and Pharisees in Matthew 23:23. The Lord sharply rebuked their attitudes about tithing. *Woe to you, teach-*

ers of the law and Pharisees, you hypocrites! You give a tenth of your spices—mint, dill and cummin. But you have neglected the more important matters of the law—justice, mercy and faithfulness. You should have practiced the latter, without neglecting the former.

The religious Pharisees appeared spiritual and godly, but they were not in right standing with God. They tithed right down to the last tiny mint leaf, but their hearts were selfish and hard.

The Lord affirms that we should tithe today, but He is concerned about our attitudes as we give to Him. In the Old Testament, God's people tithed because the law required it. Since the New Testament, we should tithe because the Lord has changed our hearts. It is a privilege to return the tithe back to Him. We tithe as an act of love for our God and also out of a heart of generosity and love for others.

Let's imagine you ask me to come to live in your house. The only stipulation is that, monthly, I need to pay 10% of all the things you provide for me. You fill the refrigerator, put gas in the car and provide all of my living expenses. It would be ridiculous for me to begin to think that everything is mine. Nothing is mine, because it belongs to you. Giving ten percent reminds me that it all belongs to you. That's what tithing is all about. The Lord's purpose for tithing is to remind us that everything we have belongs to Him.

God Will Provide

When we recognize that everything we are and have belongs to the Lord, it will be easier for us to trust the Lord to provide for us when we tithe. Even if we do not have much, God will provide when we give to Him. Giving has a way of releasing our finances. Let's learn again from the widow who gave a mite (a fraction of a penny) into the temple treasury. She sacrificially gave more than the many others who threw in large amounts because she gave all she had. *Calling his disciples to him, Jesus said, "I tell you the truth, this poor widow has put more into the treasury than all the others. They all gave out of their wealth; but she, out of her poverty, put in everything—all she had to live on" (Mark 12:43-44).*

God knows our hearts and honors our obedience in tithing. It might seem like a sacrifice, but in the long run, it helps us to become masters over our money instead of becoming a master to it.

What about those who just cannot tithe? For example, if your spouse is unsaved, you may find yourself in a dilemma. He or she may not want you to tithe. If a spouse does not agree to tithe, you cannot give something that is not yours to give. If you are the co-owner of a restaurant, you don't tithe on all the money that you take in because half of it belongs to the other owner. In the same way, you should not give away your family's money against your spouse's wishes.

Here are a few recommendations: First of all, appeal to your spouse to give some money to the church on a regular basis. Pray and allow the Holy Spirit to work in his or her heart. Perhaps you could ask the Lord for personal money you could tithe. Maybe you occasionally make some extra money at a side job—you could tithe on that personal money. Remember, God looks at our hearts and honors our obedience no matter how small our tithe may be.

Where Do We Give Our Tithes?

Where should we give our tithes? As we learned before, Malachi 3:10a says, *Bring the whole tithe into the storehouse, that there may be food in my house....*

According to this scripture, all the tithes should be placed into the storehouse. The storehouse is where spiritual food is kept to bless those who lead us, feed us and equip us for ministry. In the Old Testament, the Levites and the priests were responsible to spiritually lead and feed God's people. The tithe paid for the work of those who were set apart for the purpose of ministry to the Lord and to His people. The Levites were dependent upon the faithfulness of God's people in giving tithes to support them. *I give to the Levites all the tithes in Israel as their inheritance in return for the work they do while serving at the Tent of Meeting (Numbers 18:21).*

Since the Old Testament is a "type and a shadow" of the New Testament, the principle of where to tithe applies in the New Testament. We should tithe to the storehouse of our spiritual leaders because they are called by the Lord to minister the Word and encourage us.

Church leaders are called to "equip the saints for the work of ministry" (Ephesians 4:11-12). They need to be financially supported so that they have enough time to devote to prayer and ministering the Word of God to the saints under their care. In Acts 6:4, the leadership of the early church knew their responsibility was to single-mindedly "give their attention to prayer and the ministry of the Word."

A man once told me, "I give my tithes whenever I see a need." This man did not know it, but he was not giving a tithe, he was giving an offering. An *offering* is anything we give over and above the 10%. Tithes are the first 10% of our income given into the storehouse to provide finances to help support those who are equipping and giving spiritual leadership to the saints in the local church. *The elders who direct the affairs of the church well are worthy of double honor, especially those whose work is preaching and teaching (1 Timothy 5:17).* The word *honor* refers to *giving financially* to those who labor among us in spiritual oversight, prayer, teaching and training in the Word of God.

The Difference Between a Tithe and an Offering

As we just learned, we need to take care of the needs of those who give us spiritual oversight by giving them our tithes. As we give our tithes into the storehouse (the local church where we are fed spiritually), we are taking care of the needs of our spiritual leaders. Galatians 6:6 says that those who are taught God's Word should help provide material support for the instructors. *Anyone who receives instruction in the word must share all good things with his instructor.*

Verses 7-10 of the same chapter go on to say that if we refuse to give support to these faithful leaders, we are sowing selfishness and reaping destruction. But if we give to these leaders, it is part of "doing good to all people, especially to those who belong to the family of believers." These faithful leaders in our church are worthy of our support, and we are right in supporting them (1 Corinthians 9:14; 3 John 6-8; 1 Timothy 5:18).

Our tithe to our local church should be our first priority for giving. This kind of giving is only a place to start, however. We need to give over and beyond our tithes to many worthy causes. "Offerings" are monies given above ten percent. We should give offerings to many places and causes both within and outside our local church.

As Christians, we have a responsibility to give to the poor and needy, especially those within the church. We are encouraged to show a concern for the poor. Jesus expected that His people would give generously to the poor. Proverbs 28:27 says, *He who gives to the poor will lack nothing....*

In addition, we should also give to those who feed us spiritually from places other than our local church—perhaps through a book, a TV ministry, or another para-church ministry. These are some of the many, many places where we can give our offerings.

I have heard various radio Bible teachers say, "Do not send me your tithes; send me your offerings—that which is over and above ten percent. Your tithe belongs to your local church." I believe those Bible teachers are properly discerning the scriptures concerning the difference between tithes and offerings.

In conclusion, our tithe should go into the storehouse of the local church, and our offerings should go where we, cheerfully, voluntarily and generously, believe God is leading us to give.

Heart and Money Matters

We usually place our finances in areas that are the most important in our lives. Matthew 6:21 says that wherever we place our money, that's where our hearts will be. *For where your treasure is, there your heart will be also.*

Riches can demand the total loyalty of one's heart. That's why God tells us we must decide in our hearts to serve God and not money in Matthew 6:19-24. People who place their money in stocks, immediately check out the stock market page whenever they receive their daily newspaper. Why? Because that is where their interests lie; they are concerned about where their finances are placed. Where we give both our tithes and our offerings shows what we place high value on.

Since the Lord has called us to faithfully support our local church, it is important that we are placing our tithes in the storehouse of the local church. We encourage God's people involved in our church to faithfully tithe in obedience to the Lord, because when we tithe to our local church, our hearts are with God's people and with those who serve among us. Consequently, tithing is an issue of the heart—not a law. If we have decided within our hearts to give to our local church and its leadership, we will joyfully give our tithes to the storehouse in our church.

Giving a tithe shows we trust our leadership. When we are not willing to give a tithe, we begin, even without knowing it, to sow seeds of distrust. Tithing is a test in trust; trust in our God and trust in those the Lord has placed in spiritual leadership over our lives.

Tithing—A Test In Trust

Let's take a moment to review. A tithe, as we learned, is 10% of our income—a reminder that all we have belongs to the Lord. Offerings are gifts we give to the Lord, His people and His work that is over and above the 10% tithe. In the same way that unforgiveness opens the door for the tormenter to bring depression and confusion into people's lives (Matthew 18:34-35), robbing God of the tithe to the storehouse opens the door for the enemy to rob us. We must trust God and support His work with our tithes, according to Malachi 3:10b. *"Test me in this," says the Lord....*

God is speaking of faith and trust when He tells us to tithe to the storehouse, the place where provisions were kept for the local Levites who were serving God's people. God's people gave to the storehouse in faith because they trusted the Levites to distribute the money properly. Today the same principle of trust applies: the tithe goes into the storehouse of the local church to meet the needs of spiritual leadership who equip and encourage the church. God's plan is for those who spiritually feed and lead us to be supported by tithes. *If we have sown spiritual seed among you, is it too much if we reap a material harvest from you? If others have this right of support from you, shouldn't we have it all the more? But we did not use this right. On the contrary, we put up with anything rather than hinder the gospel of Christ. Don't you know that those who work in the temple get their food from the temple, and those who serve at the altar share in what is offered on the altar? In the same way, the Lord has commanded that those who preach the gospel should receive their living from the gospel (1 Corinthians 9:11-14).*

You may wonder, "Where should the pastor (senior elder) of a church tithe?" In some churches, the pastor tithes into the storehouse of those who give him oversight encouragement and accountability. This is often a team of spiritual leaders in the pastor's denomination or fellowship of churches.

Three Questions to Ask
1. Are You Tithing?

Malachi 3:8-12 asks the question, "Have you robbed God?" Our response usually is, "Who, me? How could I ever do that?" And then the Lord tells us how—"in tithes and offerings." Are you tithing? If not, according to the scriptures, you're robbing God. Today is the day to repent before the Lord and begin to tithe in obedience to the Word of God.

Perhaps you are disobeying the Lord by withholding tithes and offerings because you had a bad experience in the past. A young person, who is the product of a broken home, may not want to get married because of witnessing a bad marriage between his parents while growing up. However, marriage is still a wonderful plan of God. Even though you may have had bad experiences in churches where money was misused, it is still the Lord's plan for us to give our tithes and offerings into the local church. We need to press on...*forgetting what is behind and straining toward what is ahead, I press on...(Philippians 3:13-14a).*

The Lord will honor you by rebuking the devourer and opening the windows of heaven. You will also find a new sense of trust in your God and trust in those He has placed in your life who serve you in areas of spiritual leadership.

2. Are You Tithing to the Storehouse?

After God tells His people in Malachi 3 where to tithe (to the storehouse), He promises to pour out a huge blessing if they are obedient...*and see if I will not throw open the floodgates of heaven and pour out so much blessing that you will not have room enough for it (Malachi 3:10b).*

God wants to bless us, but we should tithe where He recommends—the storehouse. Are we tithing, but not to our church family? That would be like buying a hamburger at McDonalds and paying for it at Burger King! In the Old Testament, when the tithe was withheld from the storehouse, the Levites could not fulfill their role. The same is true today. In some parts of the body of Christ, pastors and other spiritual leaders are struggling financially because the tithes are being withheld in the congregations in which they serve. Consequently, they do not have enough time to effectively serve the people of God because of needing to support themselves through "tent-making" (business). The enemy can devour God's people through disobedience. Of course, some leaders, like Paul the apostle, do choose to make "tents," and this is acceptable and encouraged if the Lord has led them to do so.

What are some examples of giving our tithes to other places besides the storehouse (our church)? Giving our tithes to parachurch ministries, missionaries, evangelists or other ministries are a few examples. Although there are many missionaries, evangelists, and other Christian workers who are reputable men and women of God and need our financial support, according to my understanding of the scriptures, they should be supported through *offerings*, not through *tithes*. If we give our tithes to them, it can open the door for unbelief and lack of trust to come into our local church family. The tithe should be placed into the storehouse of our local church to be distributed to support those who give us spiritual protection and equip us to minister.

To clarify a common "tithing misunderstanding," David Wilkerson, founder of Teen Challenge and pastor of the Times Square Church in New York City, wrote in his newsletter some time back, "Concerning my statement recently about sending your tithe to our ministry, I received about 35 letters, many from pastors, lovingly reminding me that tithes belong in the local church. I totally agree. I should have clarified my statement. We have quite a number of people on our readers' list who do not attend church, sometimes because their church is shut down or they do not have a suitable church home...Believers really need to find a church home and support it. Until then, however, often my messages are the only spiritual food some people have. Overwhelmingly, those who support this ministry are faithful to support their local church, and they give us over and above their tithes."

3. Are You Tithing to the Storehouse but Designating Your Tithe Instead of Giving Freely?

Like the people in Malachi 3, are you tithing to your church, but insisting the tithe is designated for pet projects? Some believers are very willing to tithe to the storehouse, but try to control the church by withholding the tithe or a portion of the tithe, or by designating it to be used for certain things only. When we pay our taxes, we do not tell our government to spend some of the taxes on the army and another portion of our taxes to remodel a room or buy new furniture for our president or prime minister. Likewise, in our local church, when we give our tithes to the storehouse, we must trust our spiritual leadership to distribute it in a way that honors the Lord.

Excuses to Rob God

There are many reasons why Christians rob God of the tithes and offerings. One reason is simply **ignorance**. *Truly, these times of ignorance God overlooked, but now commands all men everywhere to repent (Acts 17:30 NKJ).* If you have been ignorant about this truth, you can repent (turn around) and begin to obey this spiritual truth. We serve a merciful God. He desires to bless us as we obey Him.

Some of God's people do not tithe and give offerings in direct **disobedience to the Word of God**. If we claim to know the Lord, but are not willing to obey His Word, the scriptures tell us that we are liars. We need to repent and obey the living God. *The man who says, "I know him," but does not do what he commands is a liar, and the truth is not in him (1 John 2:4).*

Another reason that some believers do not give tithes and offerings is because of **personal debt**. The Bible says in Galatians 6:7 that...*a man reaps what he sows.* The lack of giving could be part of the reason for being in debt. I read about a Christian businessman who was in debt ten times greater than his yearly income. Yet he obeyed the Lord and began to tithe and give sacrificial offerings. Within the next few years, he saw his entire financial situation turn around. God prospered him and he became a pastor of a church. The Lord began to use him to teach the truths of the Word of God regarding tithing and giving offerings and giving to hundreds of people in his community.

If you find yourself in debt, seek counsel from a trusted Christian who has wisdom in these matters. You may need to develop new habits in sound financial management. Many years ago, a Christian friend showed me how to set up a budget. Managing finances with a budget has been a real blessing to me. A budget will not control our finances, but it will give us a picture of where they are going and what the needs are.

Some people do not give tithes and offerings because they think they are **too poor**. The Lord is not concerned about the amount of money we give; He is more concerned about our attitude toward giving. Even if we have little, we can give in proportion to what God has given us. If we give nothing, we are like a farmer who eats his seed and does not have a crop for the following year. If we eat our seed (using our tithe for something other than what it was intended for), we are hindering the blessing of God in our lives.

This brings us to still another reason why many of God's people withhold their tithes and offerings. They simply **do not trust their leadership**. If we do not trust our leadership in our local church to handle the tithes we give, then we need to ask the Lord for grace to trust our spiritual leaders. If we still cannot trust them, we may be in the wrong church. 1 Corinthians 12:18 tells us that God places us in the body as He wills. It is not the church of *our* choice; it is the church of *His* choice. We need to be among a group of believers where there is a sense of faith and trust in the leadership that God has placed there.

Receive New Freedom

If you are not tithing and giving offerings, I exhort you to start today by tithing to your church. You will receive a new freedom in your life and relationship with others in the local church family in which you serve. Secondly, ask God to bless you in a way that you can give generous offerings to ministries of integrity. There are many ministries that are worthy of our gifts and offerings; however, be sure to check out where you give. The Lord holds us responsible to give offerings to reputable ministries. Do not be afraid to do your homework before giving.

Remember, tithing is a test in trust—a trust in our God who has promised to rebuke the devourer and open the windows of heaven. And it is also a trust in the spiritual leaders in our local church, as we tithe into the storehouse. The Lord desires to set us free to joyfully give our tithes and offerings to Him. And He desires to bless us as His children who obey His voice. John 8:36 tells us, *so if the Son sets you free, you will be free indeed.*

May the Lord bless you and open the windows of heaven for you as you walk in obedience to these spiritual truths.

---

[1] Dr. Bill Hamon, *Prophets And The Prophetic Movement*, (Shippensburg, PA: Destiny Image Publishers, 1990), p. 197.

Interested in more from God's Word?

- **Personal Study** Read from start to finish as an individual study program to build firm Christian foundations and develop spiritual maturity in your life.
- **Daily Devotional** Each biblical foundation book gives a month's worth of daily readings with corresponding questions.
- **Mentoring Relationship** Questions can be answered and life applications discussed as a one-on-one discipling tool.
- **Small Group Study** Study each biblical foundation in a small group setting. Each chapter has a user-friendly teaching outline.
- **Biblical Foundation Course** Use this series to teach essential biblical foundations at your church.

Titles in this series
1. Knowing Jesus Christ as Lord
2. The New Way of Living
3. New Testament Baptisms
4. Building For Eternity
5. Living in the Grace of God
6. Freedom from the Curse
7. Learning to Fellowship with God
8. What is the Church?
9. Authority and Accountability
10. God's Perspective on Finances
11. Called to Minister
12. The Great Commission

Each book has 64 pages: $4.99 each
20% off ten or more of the same title.
Complete 12 Book Set: $49.00

Foundations For Children

Creative learning for ages 4-12, patterned after the *Biblical Foundation Series*. • Step by step Bible basics learned in 48 lessons. • Fun craft or activity with each 40-60 minute lesson. • Handouts and craft ideas are photocopiable. • Lessons for home groups, children's church, family devotions, Sunday School. by Jane Nicholas, 176 pages: $17.95

Call 1-800-848-5892
www.dcfi.org   email: H2HP@dcfi.org

DOVE Christian Fellowship International presents

Spiritual Fathering & Mothering Seminar

Practical preparation for believers who want to have and become spiritual parents. Includes a manual and the book *The Cry For Spiritual Fathers & Mothers.*

Home Cell Groups Seminar

This dynamic seminar offers field-tested training to help you grow effective cell groups. For pastors and cell leaders.

Youth Cell Ministry Seminar

Learn the values behind youth cells so cell ministry does not become just another program at your church. For adult and teen leaders!

New House Church Networks Seminar

Learn how new house churches (micro-churches) are started, kept from pitfalls, and work with the rest of the body of Christ.

Elder's Training Seminar

Based on New Testament leadership principles, this seminar will equip elders to provide protection, direction and correction in the local church.

Church Planting Clinic

Designed to help you formulate a successful strategy for cell-based church planting. For those involved in church planting and those considering it.

Counseling Basics Seminar for Small Group Leaders

This seminar takes you through the basics of counseling, specifically in small group ministry. Includes a comprehensive manual.

Fivefold Ministry Seminar

A seminar designed to release healthy, effective fivefold ministry in the local church.

Marriage Mentoring Training Seminar

Trains church leaders and mature believers to help prepare engaged couples for a strong marriage foundation by using the mentoring format of the *Called Together* Manual.

Seminars held at various locations throughout the US and Canada.
For complete brochures and upcoming dates:

Call 1-800-848-5892
www.dcfi.org   email: dcfi@dcfi.org